A Scented
Christmas

Photography: Evan Bracken
Editorial Assistance: Carol Taylor
Styling: Dawn Cusick, Nancy Orban
Design: Rob Pulleyn
Production: Judy Clark, Elaine Thompson

Shot on location at the Claddagh Inn,
Hendersonville, North Carolina.

ISBN 0-8069-7471-0 Hardback
ISBN 0-8069-7470-2 Softback

10 9 8 7 6 5 4

A Sterling/Lark Book

Produced by Altamont Press, Inc.
50 College Street, Asheville, NC 28801, USA

Published in 1990 by Sterling Publishing Co., Inc.
387 Park Avenue South, New York, NY 10016

© 1990, Altamont Press

Distributed in Canada by Sterling Publishing
c/o Canadian Manda Group, P.O. Box 920, Station U
Toronto, Ontario, Canada M8Z 5P9
Distributed in the United Kingdom by Cassell PLC
Villiers House, 41/47 Strand, London WC2N 5JE, England
Distributed in Australia by Capricorn, Ltd.,
P.O. Box 665, Lane Cove, NSW 2066

A Scented Christmas

Dawn Cusick

Photography by Evan Bracken

A Sterling/Lark Book
Sterling Publishing Co., Inc., New York

Contributing Designers

Nora Blose grows an extensive variety of herbs and flowers and always enjoys finding new uses for them. (74, 75, 79, 88-top, 98, 99)

Julianne Bronder teaches floral design and basket decorating classes, along with doing commissioned works. She studied at the American Floral Art School in Chicago. (25-right, 32, 33, 34-bottom, 44, 57, 64, 65, 85, 97)

Corinne Erb is a painter, weaver, and multi-media artist who enjoys incorporating nuances from these techniques into her floral designs. She has been working with flowers for 17 years. (25-left, 42, 60, 96, 104-top, 106, 107)

Fred Tyson Gaylor is a product designer at Hanford's, Inc., a wholesale holiday accessory company in Charlotte, North Carolina. His degree is in Creative Art from the University of North Carolina. (6, 23, 40, 80-left, 81-left, 83, 90, 91)

Cynthia Gillooly enjoys creating innovative arrangements with natural materials. She owns and operates The Golden Cricket in Asheville, North Carolina. (18, 26, 76, 78, 82, 86)

Jeannette Hafner grows the flowers and greenery for her designs in her gardens in Orange, Connecticut. She teaches drying and arranging techniques as well as design classes. (7, 61, 63-bottom, 69, 81-right, 95, 101-right, 102, 111)

Carol Heller resides in Durham, Connecticut where she pursues a full-time career in bank marketing. In her spare time she works with her partner/mother, Jeannette Hafner, designing dried flower craft items. (61-center, 79, 103, 104)

Nancy McCauley gathers her own natural materials and uses traditional drying and dyeing techniques to create her arrangements. She markets her items under the name of "From Gran's . . ." in Oak Ridge, Tennessee. (28, 34-top, 36, 37, 39, 45, 50-55, 59, 63-top, 66, 68, 70-73, 77, 88, 89, 92, 93, 100-bottom, 101-left, 110)

Also thanks to . . .
Gary Albrecht, Darlene Conti (100-top), Phyllis Martin (74, 75, 99), Lowell McCauley, Mike Monroe, Sandy Mush Herb Nursery (31, 48), Tim Sigmon (46), Nicole Victoria (14, 80-top, 84)

Contents

Introduction

Christmas Memories

All of us have a very special sense of Christmas—a mental image, usually a memory from our childhoods, of what makes Christmas magical. And all of us have longed to recapture those bubbly sensations of anticipation that used to tingle under our skin as Christmas approached. But year after year, as we're bombarded with "Bah Humbugs" and heated discussions of how commercialized Christmas has become, that excitement and magic from our childhood Christmases seems more and more elusive.

As diverse as our Christmas memories may be, it is amazing to realize that we all share a very similar list of fragrances associated with Christmas. Evergreens (usually present in the form of a Christmas tree), flowers (probably because they're intrinsically beautiful and enjoy a long tradition of religious significance), herbs and spices (from the mouth-watering holiday dinners and goodies baked every year), and potpourris (because they look and smell so festive)—all embody the wonderful fragrances of our pasts.

Understanding Scent

Of the five senses—sight, smell, touch, taste, and sound—smell is probably the least understood by science. For most animals, smell is primarily a survival mechanism, while in humans smell seems to be used primarily for pleasure. Our sense of smell is strongest at birth, and steadily weakens as we age. Studies have shown that infants can distinguish their mother's breast milk from milk of other women as early as three days after birth.

Our sense of smell seems to be an intricate blend of the conscious and the subconscious. Because the conscious mind plays a role in interpreting smell, a scent that is pleasing to one person or culture may be repugnant to another. In some Mid-Eastern societies, for example, many natural body odors, such as breath, are classified as good; at the other extreme, most Westerners go to considerable effort to mask these same odors with commercially-prepared products.

On the subconscious level, our sense of smell often becomes "fatigued" when exposed to a strong odor over a long period of time—which explains why professional printers report that they don't smell their inks and why fast-food workers say they don't smell their french fries cooking.

Although the precise physiological reasons are not clearly understood by researchers, our sense of smell has been shown time and again to be linked with memory. This connection seems to work reciprocally: in other words, a memory can trigger a specific scent, or a scent can trigger a specific memory.

If you invest just a few minutes thinking about a portion of your life, (your childhood, for instance), memories of certain scents will undoubtedly surface. My own childhood memories include the gardenia bushes we played hide-and-seek under, the sweet cologne a grade school teacher wore in excess, and the salt spray from the Atlantic Ocean on breezy nights.

These same scents have often triggered mental replays of a specific moment from my past. A single whiff of the ocean sends my mind back to the nights my best friend and I walked barefoot in the surf, impatiently fluffing our hair and waiting for Prince Charming to notice us. (At the time we didn't realize that most Prince Charmings on that beach were looking for more than gawky 12-year-old schoolgirls.) When you begin investigating the scents of your own past and have these memory flashbacks, try to enjoy the many details that will also surface.

Rekindling The Spirit

The idea for this book developed one afternoon as I was bringing a carload of craft projects to a studio to be photographed. Several had been made with evergreens and spices, and it wasn't long before I was happily reliving special memories from Christmases past.

I hope you will enjoy this book on two levels: first, in making the projects; and second, in recapturing cherished Christmas memories from your own past. The book consists of five chapters, with the first chapter providing basic how-to information for making the projects and the remaining chapters presenting an exciting variety of fragrant projects to make with evergreens, flowers, herbs, spices, and potpourris.

For those of us with faraway or deceased family members, the traditional Christmas scents used in these projects may encourage our minds to take comfort in special Christmas memories. And the fragrant decorations we create this year may well trigger memories of love and cheer in the years to follow.

Happy holiday crafting . . . and, more importantly, Merry Christmas.

—Dawn Cusick

Tools & Materials

While some of the items on this page may seem foreign to you, rest assured that it will take only a few minutes of practice to learn to use them well. Pages 10-15 explain in detail how to use these tools and materials, while pages 16-21 give you directions for using them to actually make the projects in this book.

Foam

Glue Gun

Ribbon

Floral Pins

Floral Picks

Floral Tape

Wreath Base

Floral Wire
In
Spool Form

Floral
Tube

Moss

Wire Cutters

Floral Wire

Using Floral Picks

Floral picks are a versatile tool for holiday crafters. Although best known as a practical way to design with delicate flowers and greenery, picks make non-floral items, such as small bows and ribbon loops, easy to work with also.

How To Pick An Item
Hold the stem and the pick together, making sure there's enough stem to reach the top of the pick and that the flower (or other item) is above the wire.

Begin tightly wrapping the wire around the stem and the pick. At the point where the wire connects with the pick, make several extra turns with the wire.

Continue spiraling the wire down the stem until the wire ends. If desired, clip the stem at the end of the wire so the pick will perforate your base easier.

Items without a stem or other vertical area to wire the pick to can also be picked by hot-gluing the flat end of the pick to the item and then inserting into the base as usual. Generally, floral picks are sold in inexpensive bunches. They are available in green, brown, or their natural wood color. Choose the color that will blend best with the materials you'll be wiring. (Greenery, for instance, would obviously call for green picks.)

Picking Bunches
Arrange the items together as you would a small bouquet, and then follow the above directions.

Using Floral Wire

Bows, knickknacks, novelties, and even large bouquets of greenery can be attached to a base with floral wire. Although it's often difficult to find an inconspicuous place to wire the item, solving this problem may provide

inspiration for new designs. With a bouquet of greenery, for instance, you might cover the wire with small stems of dried flowers or ornaments.

Although more than one type of wire will work, floral wire (available in craft supply stores) is often the easiest to work with. Floral wire comes in a variety of thicknesses (referred to as "gauges") and is inexpensively priced. Thin or medium gauges of wire usually work best. If you're wiring an unusually heavy item, though, you may want to consider using a heavy gauge. For extra support, the item can be wired to the base and then reinforced with a dab of hot glue.

Wiring works well with almost every type of base, although vine bases, by their nature, offer more surface area.

How To Wire An Item

Look for an area on your item where the wire will not show or can be easily covered.

Wrap the wire around your item, positioning it so that both ends of the wire are on the back side of the item. Then tightly twist both ends of the wire together.

Choose the exact location on the base you'd like your item to appear. Holding the object tightly against the base, twist the wires together again until the tension is tight. Reinforce with hot glue if necessary.

Using Floral Foam

Floral foam is one of the most flexible design tools for creating everlasting floral gifts. The foam can be purchased in a variety of pre-cut shapes (cones, balls, hearts, etc.), or you can buy large blocks and cut them to the exact shape you need with a serrated knife.

Evergreens and flowers with tough, angular-cut stems can be inserted directly into the foam, while those with weak stems may need to be picked first.

The arrangement below demonstrates successful use of floral foam, pins, and mosses. The proof? None of them is visible in the completed arrangement.

Using Mosses & Pins

Many crafters choose to cover their floral foam with moss before decorating to prevent bare foam from disrupting the natural look of the design. A moss-covered base also provides a better surface area for hot-gluing items.

A variety of mosses can be purchased at floral and craft supply stores or gathered yourself outdoors. If you choose to gather your own moss, you may need to microwave it for a few minutes to kill any small insects living in the moss.

Moss can be attached to floral foam with floral pins, water-based glue, or hot glue. Since some foams will melt when exposed to hot glue, it's a good idea to test a small area of your foam before you begin.

Using Glue Guns

If, like most of us, you find yourself short of leisure time during the holiday season, then you will truly appreciate the speed and flexibility of a glue gun. If you don't already own one, you'll be surprised to discover how inexpensive (under ten dollars) they are and how little time (under ten minutes) it takes to master them.

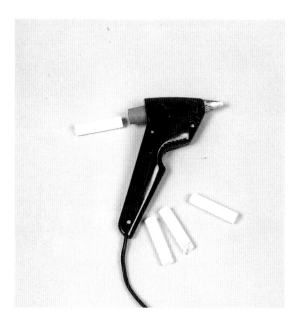

Working Tips

● While your glue gun is heating up, spread a protective layer of newspaper over your work area. If your glue gun does not have a stand, find a glass plate or other non-flammable item to rest it on.

● You may notice strands of glue that resemble spider webs. Don't worry about them as you're working—they'll easily pull off later.

● When working with foam, test a small surface of the foam to make sure the hot glue won't melt it. If melting does occur, use floral pins to cover the foam with moss and then glue the floral materials to the moss.

● Hold larger items in place for at least a minute after gluing to ensure proper bonding. Extremely large or heavy items may need to be attached with heavy-gauged wire and then hot-glued for reinforcement.

● Unplug your glue gun as soon as you've finished using it and never leave an unsupervised child near a glue gun.

● If you haven't purchased a glue gun yet, or if you burn yourself often with your current glue gun, consider investing in a "warm melt" glue gun. While the glue in these guns does get hot enough to melt, it does not get hot enough to cause severe burns.

Opposite page

While it took the maker of this wreath several hours to create the design, actually securing the materials to the base took less than 20 minutes with a glue gun. (See page 107 for more detailed directions to make this wreath.)

Making Wreaths

If you've never made a wreath before, you may be surprised to discover that wreathmaking is one of those crafts that looks difficult but is actually quite easy. Decorating materials are simply attached to a base all the way around the base until the wreath is completed.

Following is a list of popular decorating materials: evergreens, flowers (dried, fresh, silk, and parchment paper), tree ornaments, bows, ribbons, herbs, spices, potpourri, and knickknacks.

There are three basic ways to attach materials to a base: picking, hot-gluing, and wiring. (See pages 10, 14, and 11, respectively, for how-to directions.) Each method has its own strengths and limitations, and you may sometimes find that a combination of methods is the best solution. **Picking** is commonly used with dried flowers and ribbon loops. Straw, moss, and foam bases accommodate picks well. With vine bases, you may need to place a dab of hot glue on the end of the pick before inserting. **Hot-gluing** is the obvious choice for small items—such as spices or dried flower heads—that can not be picked or wired. Hot glue is often used to fill in bare spots or add design accents after other attachment methods have been used. **Wiring** offers a fast way to add craft novelties and other unusual items to a base. The challenge with wiring, of course, is finding an unobtrusive place to hide the wire. Heavier items may need to be reinforced with hot glue after wiring.

Dried flowers (and other design materials) should be picked into the base at an angle and that same angle should be maintained all the way around the base until the wreath is completed.

Bases

Every wreath begins with a base, and the three most common types are shown. Bases are available in a wide range of sizes in craft supply stores, and they are generally quite inexpensive. Designer bases, such as the cinnamon-covered base on page 97, are becoming increasingly creative.

Some bases, such as vine bases, are so attractive that you may decide to let part of the base show. Other bases, such as foam bases, should be covered with ribbon or moss before using. Straw bases are also popular. They are often sold with a layer of green plastic around them which many people leave on, while others remove it. Straw bases may also be covered with moss if desired.

Making Garlands & Swags

Garlands

Almost nothing can match the beautiful simplicity and quiet elegance of a holiday garland. Although usually quite expensive to purchase, they are surprisingly simple to make.

Because you'll need an ample supply of background material, be sure to choose something you have easy access to or can purchase inexpensively. (If you have a room full of dried artemisia from a summer garden, for instance, then artemisia would be a good choice.) Since you will need very few accent materials, though, they can be as rare or expensive as you like.

Method A: Used when working with a long-stemmed, sturdy background material, such as the cedar shown above.

Place one branch of cedar on top of a second branch near its end. Secure the two together with medium- to heavy-gauged floral wire. Continue securing branches together in this manner until the garland is the desired length.

Method B: Used when working with more delicate materials, such as dried flowers and herbs.

Cut a piece of heavy-gauged wire to the length you'd like the finished garland to be. Trim stems to equal lengths and arrange together in small bouquets (four to seven stems). Hold a single bouquet against the base wire and secure by making several loops around with clear fishing line or thin-gauged wire. Continue attaching bouquets until the garland is finished, positioning each successive bouquet to cover the stems of the previous bouquet.

Add accent materials (ornaments, ribbons, flowers, etc.) with hot glue.

Swags

The swags featured in this book are simply lush, fragrant bouquets which have been secured at their stems with floral wire and then hung upside down as wall decorations.

Perhaps the most accessible swag materials during the holiday season are Christmas tree clippings. After being arranged in a bouquet, they can be embellished with dried flowers, tree ornaments, or treasured holiday keepsakes.

Once the bouquet and its accents have been arranged and wired together, a ribbon or bow is usually attached at the top of the swag to hide the wire. Note: Tree ornaments, knickknacks, and other accents can be hot-glued into the evergreens or secured under the wire.

Arrange the background material (i.e. evergreens, eucalyptus, etc.) in a fan shape. Secure with medium-gauged floral wire.

Place stems of accent materials (or additional stems of background material if a thicker swag is desired) and secure with a second wire. Cover the wire with a bow or ribbon. Add ornaments or knickknacks if desired. (See page 34-top for a sample.)

Making Arrangements

Like most artists, florists work very hard to make what they do appear very easy. Many of us have avidly watched the carefree way in which a florist creates an arrangement, only to be disappointed when we try to mimic them at home. As easy as they make it look, though, florists actually work under a fairly rigid set of design principles.

The first basic principle a beginner needs to learn is shape. The next time you're in a florist's shop or browsing through a magazine, pay careful attention to the shapes of arrangements. Oval, round, and triangular shapes are the three easiest designs for beginners to work with. The following steps will guide you through your first arrangement.

Decide on the shape you would like to make (i.e. oval, round, or triangular) and create a mental image of this shape in your mind as you look at your container. Beginning with a stem of greenery, insert the stem in the place you envision to be the top focal point of your arrangement. (With a triangular shape, the top focal point would obviously be much higher than with a round or oval shape.)

Next, create the remaining perimeters of the shape by inserting greenery all the way around the base.

Begin by cutting a piece of floral foam to the shape of your chosen container. Allow the foam to protrude slightly over the·container so that stems can be inserted horizontally, and anchor it well inside the container. Secure with wire, hot glue, or floral tape if necessary.

The same method described above is now repeated with flowers: insert a top central flower at the highest point of your shape, again relying on your mental image to guide you; then establish outer perimeters with additional flowers. Note that tree ornaments and props may replace these "focal flowers" for holiday arrangements.

Now that the perimeters of the arrangement have been firmly established, fill in the remaining space with additional stems of flowers. Last, take a final look at your arrangement to make sure there are no bare spots where foam is visible. If so, cover with a small piece of moss or additional greenery.

Designer Tips

● Flowers and greenery with sturdy stems can be inserted directly into the foam after cutting their stems at an angle; weak-stemmed items can be wired to floral picks and inserted that way.

● For a good arrangement, depth is crucial, so try to be conscious of inserting some flowers deeper than others.

● A good arrangement will draw the eye inward, so try to arrange darker colored flowers in the center to add depth.

● Generally, place smaller flowers and buds at the top focal point and outer edges; place larger flowers towards the bottom.

● The shape of an arrangement should echo the shape of its container.

● Try to design your arrangement at the same height from which it will be displayed. The arrangement displayed on an eight-foot mantel will not look the same as it did at eye level.

● When working with fresh-cut materials whose beauty you'd like to preserve, substitute oasis foam for floral foam. The sponge-like quality of oasis allows it to absorb enough water to nourish flowers and greenery for several days.

An example of an arrangement with a triangular shape.

Making Topiaries & Trees

For beginners, the easiest way to make a topiary is to purchase a pre-assembled form in a craft store and then simply decorate it. If you have trouble locating one, though, you can make your own form by securing a long stick in a foam ball and anchoring it in a piece of foam cut to fit a pot or basket. Larger topiaries may need to be weighted with stones or plaster.

To decorate the topiary, cover the foam ball with dried flowers, herbs, spices, evergreens, or ribbons. These materials can be attached to the ball with floral picks or hot glue. Many designers choose to decorate the base of the topiary also.

Small trees make a simple, inexpensive project and are also a good way to use up leftover materials. (See page 111 for an example.)

Simply cover a cone-shaped piece of foam with moss (using floral pins or craft glue) and then decorate in a spiral design with evergreens, spices, herbs, or dried flowers. Trees can also be completely covered with these materials, although the additional weight may mean you have to anchor the tree in a small basket or container.

Tussie mussies have become increasingly popular in the last several years, probably as a result of a trend towards larger, more formal weddings. These remnants of 18th-century Victorian days are a lovely way to decorate small tables around the home. Miniature tussie mussies can be secured in small doilies and used as tree ornaments or package decorations.

Tussie mussies are usually made with dried flowers or herbs. They can be purchased in craft stores or dried at home fresh-cut from the garden.

Begin by choosing a center flower. Dried roses are popular choices, although many beautiful alternatives exist. Secure a short length of thin-gauged floral wire to the center flower by inserting it up through the stem and into the bud. Make a small hook in the top of the wire and pull it back down through the flower until it anchors in place.

Encircle the center flower with small stems of dried flowers. (Baby's breath is shown in the photo here.) Hold these flowers against the center flower's wire and secure them together by wrapping floral tape around them at a slight angle. To avoid bulkiness, do not wrap the tape all the way down the stem. Continue creating small bouquets using the above method until you have enough bouquets to make the size tussie mussie you'd like.

Arrange all of the miniature bouquets around the center flower's bouquet. Holding them tightly together with your left hand, secure them together with more floral tape, beginning as close to the base of the bouquets as possible and wrapping down about four inches. Trim the stems evenly with tin shears. Cover all of the floral tape with a thin width of lace, wrapping at the same angle as the tape. Secure with hot glue as needed.

Finish the tussie mussie with lace gathers (secured with hot glue), ribbon streamers, or a lace doily that's been dipped in fabric stiffener.

Evergreens

This Christmas dinner centerpiece was created by inserting fragrant dried flowers, artificial fruits, and glycerin-preserved evergreens into a rectangular base of floral foam.

The candles were inserted first using small plastic candle holders. Available in craft supply stores, these specially designed holders are tapered to a sharp point, allowing for easy insertion into the floral foam and preventing fire hazards.

The edges of the foam base were then picked with fraser fir and arborvitae to form a background. The flowers (dried lavender, heather, and roses) and the fruits were then picked into the remaining space. Last, small loops of ribbon were picked into the foam.

Evergreens have played an integral role in winter holidays and celebrations since the beginning days of civilization. Early Christians viewed evergreens as a symbol of fertility because they seemed to flourish during otherwise barren months; in the 17th and 18th centuries, evergreens were so revered that serving platters were covered with a layer of evergreens before placing foods on them.

Most of the projects in this chapter were created with small branches and clippings from a variety of fragrant conifers (i.e. firs, hemlocks, pines, spruces, and cedars). As you begin paying more attention to evergreens, you will undoubtedly notice their interesting variations in fragrance and texture. The fragrance of some evergreens is quite spicy, while in others it closely resembles that of a citrus peel. Textures range from flat and dull to three-dimensional and glossy.

Rest assured, though, that you needn't be an evergreen expert or live in the woods to make these projects. If you live in a city, visit local Christmas tree lots and ask if you can buy a bundle of clippings. Friends and neighbors are also good sources, as well as florists who usually order large quantities of evergreens for their holiday arrangements.

The projects can be made with fresh-cut evergreens or with evergreens that have been preserved with glycerin. Both types look and smell wonderful, but the fresh evergreens will begin to brown after a few weeks (which you may not find objectionable if you plan to throw the project away after Christmas) and the glycerin-preserving technique requires several weeks of advanced planning. (See page 30 for glycerin-preserving directions.)

The stems of most evergreens are sturdy enough to insert directly into floral foam. For easier insertion, though, you may want to cut the stems at a slight angle. Evergreens also make a wonderful background material for decorative accents such as tree ornaments and holiday knickknacks.

Right

This lightweight holiday topiary can be moved from room to room, wherever you feel the need for some holiday cheer. The topiary also makes an ideal gift for someone in a hospital or a nursing home who doesn't have much space.

The topiary began with a store-bought double topiary frame that had been hot-glued at its base to the inside of a small basket. The top ball was first decorated with tinted reindeer moss secured in place with floral pins. The red velvet bow was picked in next and its streamers were allowed to drape over the ball.

The larger, middle ball was decorated by picking in stems of glycerin-preserved fraser fir, cinnamon sticks, and artificial berries. Small pieces of reindeer moss were picked in last to hide any bare spots.

Last, the base of the topiary was covered with more reindeer moss and several small velvet bows were picked in back to back.

*C*reated with only a
few simple materials, this
striking garland moves
easily from the mantel to
the center of the dinner
table.

The garland was made
by wiring ten-inch (25-cm.)
branches of glycerin-
preserved cedar to a base of
heavy-gauged wire. Four
florist's water tubes were
then filled with water, hot-
glued into the cedar, and
filled with yellow roses.
Small plastic tree orna-
ments were hot-glued in
next and a length of festive
French ribbon was looped
through the garland as a
final touch.

Tip: If some or all of
your water tubes are visible
through the greenery,
consider hot-gluing a few
stems of dried flowers
around them. In this
garland, German statice
was used to conceal the
water tubes.

*M*any crafters avoid making formal arrangements because they don't know where to find formal glass containers; or, if they have seen something special, they'd rather not invest a lot of money for a seasonal item.

Surprisingly, though, most of us have some absolutely beautiful bowls and containers safely stored in a china cabinet that would be perfect for a holiday centerpiece.

For the arrangement shown here, an antique ironstone vegetable bowl, handed down from a fondly-remembered grandmother, made an ideal vessel for this arrangement. (After Christmas, the arrangement can be removed and the bowl returned to its usual storage place.)

The arrangement was made with glycerin-preserved spruce and magnolia leaves, dried Mexican sage, German statice, sumac, artemisia, and dyed oak leaf hydrangea.

Designer Tip

As any weekend gardener can tell you, hydrangea is not naturally a bright Christmas red.

It is, however, a very simple process to add color to dried flowers. Simply prepare a dye bath by following the directions on a package of powdered dye. Then dip several dried hydrangea heads in the bath until you're satisfied with the color. Last, hang them upside down until dry.

Other easily-dried flowers, such as yarrow, goldenrod, and statice, can also be dyed.

Amazingly, it takes only a few branches of fraser fir to emit the wonderful fragrance of Christmas. The top of the wreath shown here was created by picking stems of dried German statice and fresh fraser fir into a 16-inch (41-cm.) straw base. The bottom arrangement was created with dried feverfew, sumac, strawflowers, bay leaves, ivy, sweet Annie, silver king artemisia, fraser fir, and German statice.

Preserving with Glycerin

To glycerin-preserve an evergreen, fill a small container with three parts water to one part glycerin. Make several angular cuts in the evergreens' stems and stand them in the liquid. As time passes, the evergreens will absorb the glycerin mixture through their stems. The process usually takes about two weeks, but you should let the evergreens' appearance dictate the exact amount of time. Slight color changes are normal, with most evergreens darkening in tone. If you're interested in experimenting, small amounts of green powdered dye can be added to the glycerin mixture.

Several common varieties of leaves also do well with glycerin-preserving, although their fleshier stems may need a higher glycerin-to-water ratio.

This small eucalyptus swag hangs beautifully on the inside closet door of a guest room, freshening the air and providing a surprise reminder of the Christmas season each time the door is opened.

The swag was made by arranging ten stems of eucalyptus in a fan shape and then securing them loosely together with floral wire. Next, stems of dried teal ruskus were inserted under the wire and the wire was then tightened to hold the arrangement in place. Last, a lace bow was wired to the arrangement, creatively covering the previously-used wire.

*S*uccessfully decorating a bathroom for the holiday season is a real challenge: too much seems gaudy, while too little goes unnoticed. The basket shown here, though, adds just the right amount of festivity and fragrance.

The basket was decorated by first hot-gluing short stems of glycerin-preserved fraser fir around the rim. A length of lace ribbon was then looped around the fir and hot-glued randomly to help maintain its shape.

The bow was hot-glued on next, and each side was accented with a simple pinon pine cone hot-glued in place. Last, the basket was filled with more cones and fir.

The Christmas trees which we see as such an integral part of our contemporary holiday celebrations enjoy a long and fascinating history, crossing several cultures and defying pedigree. Below are some of the more interesting tales of the Christmas tree's origin.

- Medieval story tellers wrote tales of evergreen trees that were decorated in the winter months to symbolize the tree of temptation in the Garden of Eden.
- Martin Luther cut down the first Christmas tree, brought it inside his home, and decorated it to replicate the star-filled skies of Bethlehem on Christmas eve.
- The Christmas tree tradition was born in Germany, and brought to Europe when Princess Helen of Mecklenburg married the Duke of Orleans in 1837. Seven years later, the trend had crossed to England, and finally worked its way to America with immigrating Germans.

*E*asily moved from room to room, hanging bouquets are a versatile way to add fragrance throughout your home.

This bouquet was made with spruce, cedar, sumac, dried roses, pine cones, dyed wild yarrow, silver king artemisia, and glass tree ornaments.

When the holiday season has passed, just remove the ornaments and add a new bow for a beautiful winter bouquet.

*S*hort stems of fraser fir were hot-glued under the bow of a package to create an enticing, aromatic gift.

Tip: Empty clothing boxes can also be decorated and used to adorn doors and walls around the house.

Floral tree ornaments are an ideal way to use up leftover scraps from bigger projects, and with careful packing they can be used year after year.

The ornaments shown here were created by hot-gluing dried flowers to ordinary ornaments and miniature vine wreath bases.

In many Scandinavian countries, placing a standing bunch of wheat outdoors for the birds is a cherished tradition.

You can make your bouquet "stand" by wiring two bunches of wheat together about a fourth of the way down from the top and then twisting one bunch behind the other until it stands upright.

Wheat bouquets are often so lovely that you may find yourself making two: one for the birds and one to display in your home. The bouquet shown here was decorated with cedar, dried German statice, small ornaments, and a red velvet bow. All items were hot-glued in place.

This large festoon emanates fragrance from the branches of glycerin-preserved arborvitae and fraser fir that were used as a background for silk fruits and dried flowers.

The festoon's base was cut from thin plywood, and can be custom-sized to fit over a fireplace or other special location. All of the materials were hot-glued directly to the base, with the evergreens attached first. The silk fruits included grapes, peaches, and pomegranates, while the flowers included dried roses, heather, lavender, and silk Madonna lilies.

Since this project could

be quite expensive if you had to pay full price for all of the silk fruits at a craft store, you may want to substitute some inexpensive filler material, such as wheat stalks, bows, old tree ornaments, etc.

While evergreens provided the enticing fragrance of this wreath, flowers and herbs from a summer garden provided the bright, cheerful colors.

Handfuls of balsam branches were first attached to a 16-inch (41-cm.) straw base with floral pins. A length of green ribbon was then looped around the wreath and hot-glued in place every few inches (eight cm.).

The dried flowers, herbs, and greenery—boxwood, princess pine, tree ferns, roses, carnations, caspia, sweet Annie, statice, zinnias, eucalyptus, lamb's ear, pussy willows, straw-flowers, cockscomb, artemisia, nutmeg, and star anise—were then hot-glued into the balsam.

After a few weeks, the fresh balsam dried naturally on the wreath and its wonderful fragrance remains.

Designer Tip

If you enjoy gardening but have never tried to dry your own flowers, we hope the beauty of the dried flowers in this wreath will encourage you to try.

Many flowers will dry by simply hanging them upside down in a moisture-free environment for several weeks.

Some flowers, such as roses, dry best when picked in the early stages of their blooming cycle. Other flowers, such as annual statice, will dry well during almost every stage of their blooming cycles.

For best results, avoid harvesting flowers when they're still wet from the morning dew or rain.

In Australia, eucalyptus trees are widely cultivated for their hard wood. In America, though, eucalyptus is appreciated for its ornamental appeal and refreshing fragrance.

Eucalyptus stems (available by the bunch in many craft stores) are sturdy enough to insert directly into floral foam, and their leaves can be attractively spray-painted with gold, silver, or copper. Over 200 varieties grow in temperate climates around the world.

Table wreaths are a lovely way to display favorite antiques and collectables, such as this gold lantern. Since most wreaths are several inches high, your chosen item can be elevated several inches for better proportions.

Long stems of eucalyptus were first trimmed to three-inch lengths (eight-cm.) and then picked into a small foam base. Three satin bows were then picked into the base, and small pine cones were hot-glued in as accents. As a special touch, the wreath was spray-painted with gold glitter for a holiday effect.

A simple wall basket was spray-painted red to create a container for this aromatic arrangement. The pocket of the basket was then filled with floral foam, and the materials—glycerin-preserved magnolia leaves and cedar, dyed oak leaf hydrangea, daisies, cinnamon sticks, and glass tree ornaments—were simply arranged and inserted into the foam.

While the base of this large table centerpiece is more time-consuming to construct than that of a smaller arrangement, the larger size of the design materials tends to make up for any lost time.

The base was created by covering a large rectangle of plywood with a layer of green felt using hot glue. Tip: Since the size of your rectangle will be about one-fourth of the final arrangement's size, be sure to do your math first to avoid disappointment.

Next, a second rectangle was cut to the same size as the plywood from floral foam and hot-glued to the felt-covered base. The outer perimeters of the arrangement were then created with dried palms and glycerin-preserved cedar branches.

Large hemlock cones and sumac heads were then picked into the foam, and additional stems of cedar and palm filled in any remaining bare spots. Last, delicate stems of dried baby's breath and feverfew were hot-glued into the arrangement.

A *fragrant assortment of Christmas tree clippings*
was combined with colorful sumac heads, red peppers,
sweet Annie, bay leaves, and cinnamon sticks for a
dinner centerpiece. All of the items were attached to
floral picks and then inserted into a square of floral foam.

If you like, gold and silver glass tree ornaments can
be scattered around the centerpiece or tucked into the
evergreens.

Gold and pewter horns, available inexpensively in larger craft supply stores, form ideal bases for festive decorations.

For the arrangement shown here, a piece of corrugated cardboard was first cut to a half-moon shape, extending about six inches (15 cm.) from the horn. A base of glycerin-preserved cedar was then hot-glued to the cardboard, and the backside of the cardboard was hot-glued to the horn.

Pine cones, eucalyptus, glass tree ornaments, glycerin-preserved spruce, dried German statice, roses, and lavender were then layered on top of the cedar and hot-glued in place.

If the back of your arrangement will show, it can be covered with greenery or a piece of gift wrap.

With a little forethought and planning, you can surprise everyone on your gift list with a personalized fragrant arrangement. The materials for this project cost less than five dollars, making it an ideal gift for neighbors, schoolteachers, postmen, and other special friends.

A plain, inexpensive wicker basket was first spray-painted white and then decorated with red velvet ribbon (attached with hot glue) and a stenciled cardinal design. Next the arrangement was created with cedar, dried mirandy roses, silver king artemisia, German statice, German myrtle, glycerin-preserved magnolia leaves, small glass tree ornaments, and red velvet bows.

(Tip: Instead of stenciling a holiday design onto the basket, you might consider clipping holiday pictures and scenes from magazines, gluing them to the basket, and applying a thin coat of clear varnish to finish.)

This pewter horn table display adds elegance and fragrance to any room, yet is amazingly simple to make. A piece of heavy cardboard was first cut in the shape of the arrangement and hot-glued to the horn. Glycerin-preserved cedar and spruce, dried German statice, mirandy roses, canella berries, gypsophilia, and small Christmas balls were then arranged and hot-glued to the cardboard. (The back of the arrangement can be covered with a festive wrapping paper or a layer of cedar if it will show.)

*T*he natural colors and fragrances in this wreath were created with dried canella berries, German statice, gypsophilia, dyed yarrow, dusty miller, pearly everlasting, glycerin-preserved fraser fir, and an assortment of pine cones. All of the items were picked onto a 16-inch (41-cm.) straw base.

The wreath could be further embellished with a bow and/or tree ornaments if desired.

*T*his colorful door swag was made by wiring a large bunch of eucalyptus in its center and then attaching a festive bow. Small pieces of dried caspia were then dabbed with hot glue at the base of their stems and inserted under the bow. Christmas ornaments could easily be added if you desire.

Flowers

One of the most popular holiday flower fragrances, that of the rose, has been delighting people for centuries. Near-Eastern folklore has it that mosque walls were painted with rose water to honor Saldin's visit to Jerusalem in 1147. Early Greek and Roman civilizations were also enraptured by the rose and its fragrance.

As any rose lover will tell you, each type of rose has its own distinct scent, and these variations are often so subtle that language

A cornucopia of holiday flowers can be enjoyed as a wall hanging or placed on any table in the home to add holiday cheer.

This cornucopia was made by dipping a lace doily into fabric stiffener and rolling it into the desired shape. After the stiffener had dried, the inside back of the doily was brushed with craft glue and several stems of greenery were pushed against it. Remaining flowers and greenery were simply inserted into the leftover space, with no additional glue needed.

defies describing them. Although many rose experts claim they have pinpointed a particular rose scent—spices, honey, fruits, almonds, and verbena to name just a few—most of us simply classify the fragrance as "sweet."

The roses and other flowers you choose for your Christmas arrangements can be fresh or dried. Fresh flowers offer the advantage of a stronger scent, while arrangements with dried flowers can be used year after year. Fresh flowers will retain their beauty longer if inserted into small water tubes (called floral tubes) which are then inserted directly into an arrangement.

Although some dried flowers are fragrant, you may wish to strengthen or add fragrance by adding a small drop of essential oil (see essential oils, page 83) to their petals. Silk and paper can also be fragranced with essential oils.

*S*urprise your holiday guests by placing this tall topiary in their room and surrounding it with beautifully wrapped and decorated packages.

The topiary was made by securing the base in a large verdigris basket (highlighted with gold spray-paint) and then hot-gluing sheet moss around both foam balls.

Dried rosebuds, heather, globe amaranth, nutmegs, statice, cinnamon sticks, bay leaves, carnations, eucalyptus, pepper berries, and grape vine tendrils were then arranged and hot-glued to the moss-covered balls.

Last, the basket was filled with evergreen clippings and a large French ribbon was added. When the holiday season has passed, remove the topiary to a clay pot, add a colorful paper bow, and fill in with additional flowers.

Create a Victorian atmosphere in your home this year by decorating packages with miniature tussie mussies and placing small topiaries under the tree or on small tables around your home.

The topiaries were made by hot-gluing an assortment of dried flower heads and eucalyptus to small topiary forms and then decorating the stems with greenery and vines. The dried flowers included globe amaranth, roses, straw-flowers, and tinted pepper grass.

This colorful floral swag can be custom-made to fit over a mantel, doorway, or other special location.

A length of heavy wire was first cut to the approximate size of the finished swag. Beginning at each end of the wire and working towards the center, small bundles of artemisia, eucalpytus, and juniper cut to about three inches (seven cm.) were then attached to the base with clear fishing line.

Once the base was covered with artemisia, an assortment of colorful dried flowers—celosia, globe amaranth, hydrangea, delphinium, larkspur, strawflowers, pepper grass, and pepper berries—was hot-glued into the swag.

After the holiday season passes, remember to store the swag carefully in paper, not plastic.

*A*lthough bright Christmas reds and greens usually seem festive around the house, they often clash with the more subtle colors of many bathrooms' decor. The holiday decorations shown here used pale pinks and greens to create a holiday look, while the heart-shaped soaps emit a soothing bayberry scent.

The basket arrangement was made by first cutting a piece of floral foam to fit the inside of the basket and hot-gluing it in place. One end of medium-gauged wire was then inserted through a hole that had been pre-drilled into each soap; the other end of the wire was inserted into the foam at varying angles. The arrangement was then filled out with stems of dried sugar bush, baby's breath, and parchment paper foliage—all commercially tinted in colors that matched the soaps. Last, the bow was wired to the basket's handle.

The coordinating wreath was made by wrapping a wooden base with a narrow satin ribbon all the way around. A length of lace ribbon was then used to create sections. (Note: The ribbon can be stapled or hot-glued on the back side of the base if necessary.) The soaps and the bow were then hot-glued to the base and a loop was made at the top of the wreath for hanging.

*O*ften evoking the mood of their Victorian heritage, tussie mussies are becoming popular Christmas decorations for coffee tables, bedroom dressers, and china cabinets.

The tussie mussie shown here was made from dried pearly everylasting, bleached oak leaf hydrangea, dyed wild yarrow, pink roses, oregano, annual statice, cockscomb, and dianthus. A generous use of ribbon streamers and gathered lace added a professional touch.

This page

*S*mall scraps of dried flowers attached with hot glue to miniature wreath bases and holiday knick-knacks created distinctive tree ornaments.

Opposite page
  Above: Miniature tussie mussies add Victorian elegance to Christmas trees when nestled in their fragrant branches.
  Below: Dried flowers, greenery, and ribbons were secured to glass tree ornaments with craft glue.

*T*his elegant tussie mussie was designed as a tree topper, although a creative decorator could probably find numerous other places around the home to display it.

The tree topper was made in the same way as a regular tussie mussie (see page 21 for general directions), and the long streamers were attached last to the back of the arrangement with a thin-gauged floral wire.

The flowers included dried roses, bleached gypsophilia, pearly ever-lasting, dyed oak leaf hydrangea, and wormwood. Artifical red berries, redwood cones, and glycerin-preserved cedar tips were also used.

If you plan to re-use the topper next Christmas, be sure to store it in paper, not plastic, to prevent the dried flowers from re-absorbing moisture.

Miniature tussie mussies, made the same way
as their larger counterparts, can be used to decorate
packages, trim the tree, or just scatter around the home
in out-of-the-way places.

While most garlands are made on straight wire bases, they can also be made on a wire base that's been curved, allowing you to custom-fit a garland to a specific place in your home.

For the garland shown here, a length of coat hanger wire was curved to match the U-shape of the mirror. The dried flowers—sweet Annie, gypsophilia, lavender, carnations, heather, and dyed oak leaf hydrangea—were then wired onto the base.

Last, the bow was tied in the center and the streamers looped down each side, with a dab of hot glue used occasionally to help hold the loops in place.

Note: Some larger craft supply stores sell wire bases in U-shapes.

Potpourris

When looking for ways to display your potpourris, try to think beyond the traditional glass bowl. The lanterns shown here were decorated with lace doilies and red ribbons, and then filled with a fragrant potpourri.

Gift packages decorated with ribbons, tulle, feathers, and knickknacks were fragranced with small potpourri ornaments.

Right: Two potpourri-filled tulle bags were tied with red ribbon were hot-glued around the teddy bears. Candy canes and additional ribbon curls were added as special touches.

Below: Heart-shaped foam pieces were covered with a layer of craft glue, rolled in potpourri, and then creatively nestled in feathers and tulle.

Fragrant, colorful potpourris are beautiful when displayed in special glass bowls. The potpourri shown here was made by mixing the ingredients below in a large, airtight container and stirring them every few days.

"Nancy's All-Natural Potpourri"

1½ cup dried rosebuds
1 cup dried lavender
½ cup dried peppermint leaves
½ cup chopped bay leaves
1 cup dried chamomile
½ cup dried lemon verbena
1 cup dried cornflowers
1 cup dried oak moss
1 cup dried sweet woodruff
½ cup cloves
¾ cup whole allspice
3 tablespoons cinnamon powder
3 tablespoons ground nutmeg.

Over the centuries potpourri has appealed to a variety of cultures for a variety of reasons. Today, potpourri is becoming increasingly popular, and appeals to a diverse group of people. Gardeners relish potpourri as a way to preserve the beauty of their spring and summer gardens. Grocery shoppers purchase commercially-made bags of potpourri as substitutes for aerosol air fresheners. Still others use colorful potpourris as a practical way to display cherished crystal and china glassware.

Making your own potpourris (discussed in the following pages) can be as simple or complicated as you choose. Do not allow yourself to become frustrated in trying to duplicate the exact ingredients of the recipes from this chapter. Instead, use the recipes as a guide, deleting ingredients that are difficult to find and adding ingredients whose fragrances you enjoy. Remember: the only two requirements of a successful potpourri are that they be fragrant and visually attractive. Not all of the items in your potpourri need to be fragrant. Some, like small hemlock cones and acorns, can be included simply for texture and variety.

Without realizing it, you probably already have a nice variety of potpourri ingredients in and around your home. Some of these include evergreens, bay leaves, cloves, cinnamon, allspice, etc. Other ingredients can be located with just a little effort. Flower petals, for instance, can often be found in the winter by locating a friendly florist who is willing to donate his or her scraps.

(Continues on page 83)

Above

Decorating the top of a special gift package with a favorite potpourri takes only a few minutes and makes an ideal children's project.

This package was decorated by applying a thin layer of craft glue to the top of the package, and then sprinkling a layer of potpourri over the glue. The potpourri was then gently pushed into the glue with the bottom of a glass. After the craft glue had dried completely, a plaid bow was attached with hot glue.

Right

Small sachet bags made with holiday fabrics can be placed under a pillow or in a drawer and are a festive way to welcome guests. The bags can also be made in smaller sizes and used as tree ornaments or stocking stuffers.

*F*or the sachets
shown here, a cinnamon
potpourri was placed inside
the bags and then tightly sealed
with ribbon. Small fragrant
bouquets—made from dried roses,
boxwood, bay leaves, pepper berries,
and nutmegs—were then hot-glued to
the ribbon.

Tip: If your decorative materials are
fragrant, be sure their fragrance is
compatible with that of the potpourri.

*P*otpourri ornaments are simple to make and use a minimum of materials.

Above: a small foam ball was hot-glued to an ordinary ice cream cone, covered with water-based craft glue, and rolled in potpourri for a delicious look.

Right: gossamer-like gathers of tulle hold a fragrant sachet of potpourri.

Far right: small glass ornaments were filled with a colorful potpourri and decorated with flower scraps.

Recipe

ivy leaves, bay leaves,
whole nutmegs, rose petals,
balsam branches,
two drops of vanilla-
scented essential oil

Miniature vine wreaths decorated with potpourri add sparkle and charm to any holiday package.

The miniature potpourri wreaths were made by covering the top of each base with a thick layer of water-based craft glue and gently pressing the potpourri into the glue. After the glue dried, the wreaths were attached to the package with small dabs of hot glue.

The wonderful scents of potpourris can be achieved in several ways. Following is a discussion of the three most popular ways, along with the benefits and disadvantages of each.

Fragrance can easily be achieved by combining naturally fragrant items—such as evergreens, cloves, cinnamon, and citrus peels—together in different proportions until you like the scent. While these potpourris will be fragrant through the holidays, they will lose most of their fragrance by the following month.

Fragrance can also be added to potpourris by combining a few drops of essential oil with your ingredients. Essential oils are available in a variety of specialty shops, and it takes only a few drops to create a strong fragrance. When the fragrance starts to dissipate in several months, it can be rejuvenated with a few more drops of oil. You may notice that the prices of essential oils vary dramatically. These cost differences are usually based on whether the "essence" of the oil was achieved naturally or synthetically.

Another way to add fragrance is to "preserve" your potpourri's scent with a natural fixative, such as orrisroot. With this method, the potpourri's ingredients are blended with a small amount of powdered orrisroot and left in a sealed container for several weeks. While these potpourris are wonderfully fragrant, they tend to take more time and pre-planning than many of us are willing to invest during the holidays.

If none of these methods appeal to you, simply purchase a commercially-prepared bag of potpourri and embellish it with your favorite scents and decorative materials.

Tip: When your potpourri's scent begins to diminish, stir it well and then crush a few of the more fragrant ingredients.

Versatile potpourri wreaths are as lovely on a table as they are on the wall.

This centerpiece was made by covering a foam base with a thick layer of water-based craft glue and then sprinkling on the potpourri and pressing it gently in place.

Artificial crab apples and silk leaves were then arranged and hot-glued on top of the potpourri. The bowl was filled with matching potpourri after securing a candle in place with floral clay.

*I*n less than half an hour, an ordinary store-bought topiary form was converted into a shimmering remembrance of Victorian times.

After securing the foam base in a clay pot, the top ball was covered with craft glue. Small handfuls of potpourri were then sprinkled over the glue and gently pressed in place. Next, the area around the base was decorated with more pot-pourri, and gold ribbons were hot-glued in place. As a special touch, the pot was highlighted with a light layer of gold glitter spray-paint.

Recipe

red and yellow rose petals,
ferns, cinnamon sticks,
grape vine shavings,
two drops of rose-scented
essential oil

*S*elect pieces from a store-bought bag of potpourri were arranged and hot-glued around the rim of an inexpensive basket. The remainder of the potpourri was then sprinkled over a bed of evergreen clippings for a matched set.

You can personalize a commercially-prepared potpourri by adding any of the following items commonly found around the house: small pieces of evergreen clippings, bay leaves, cinnamon sticks, cloves, and flower petals.

Recipe

balsam branches, miniature hemlock, cinnamon sticks, two drops of bayberry-scented essential oil

*S*mall pieces of tulle filled with potpourri and tied with a ribbon make fragrant tree ornaments and package decorations.

For the package shown here, a light dab of hot glue secured the potpourri bags to the package, and small stems of dried German statice were hot-glued as extra touches.

*S*imple glass ornaments can be transformed easily and inexpensively into magical decorations for your home or special keepsake gifts for friends.

The ornament shown here was first filled with a colorful potpourri and then decorated with gold ribbon and small sprigs of dried flowers. A hot-glue gun made attachment fast and simple.

As wall hangings and tree ornaments, these
miniature potpourri wreaths are a simple way to add
fragrance and cheer.

The wreaths were made by covering two four-inch
(ten-cm.) foam bases with white craft glue and then
gently pressing handfuls of potpourri into the glue.
After the base was completely covered, the wreath was
decorated further with single pieces of favorite potpourri
ingredients, such as red rose petals and small evergreen
pieces.

A small bag of store-bought potpourri added color and a strawberry fragrance to this holiday wreath.

Three-fourths of a ten-inch (25-cm.) foam base was first covered with white craft glue. The potpourri was then pressed into the glue and allowed to dry.

Last, silk apples, roses, cranberries, and branches of glycerin-presrved fir were arranged and hot-glued to the bare portion of the base.

Recipe

sage, fraser fir,
dried apple slices,
assorted small nuts
and cones,
dried orange peel

*T*rimmed with silk
fruits, cinnamon stick
bundles, and miniature
potpourri baskets, this tall
silk Christmas tree makes a
thoughtful gift for someone
in a nursing home or
hospital.

The potpourri baskets
were made by cutting small
pieces of foam to fit the
inside of the baskets and
hot-gluing them in place.
The top of the foam was
then covered with a water-
based craft glue and the
potpourri was sprinkled
on top.

Recipe

bay leaves, star anise,
cinnamon sticks, cloves,
rose petals, dried rosemary

Herbs & Spices

Simmers are an easy way to add holiday fragrance to your home. About half an hour before you expect guests to arrive (or when you'd just like to enjoy the fragrance yourself), bring the simmer recipe to a boil and then reduce the heat to low and allow the fragrance to fill the room.

Tip: Other rooms can be fragranced with a simmer by placing the steaming pan on a hot plate. Simmers can usually be re-used several times, and you can often rejuvenate them by adding additional ingredients.

"Nancy's Evergreen Simmer"

Thoroughly mix the following ingredients in a bowl. Next, combine the mixture with one cup of water, bring to a boil, and allow to simmer.

¼ cup mixed dry "pine" needles (Cedar, white pine and spruce all work well.)
¼ cup hemlock cones (or other small cones)
1 tablespoon cloves
1 tablespoon whole allspice
2 tablespoons cut up, dried orange peel
¾ tablespoon cinnamon
¾ tablespoon ground nutmeg
1-2 broken pieces of cinnamon bark

The alluring appeal of this fragrant garland of dried herbs illustrates why herbs have fascinated humankind for hundreds of years.

A piece of heavy-gauged wire cut to the length of the desired finished piece was first wrapped with green floral tape. Small bundles of artemisia cut in four-inch (ten-cm.) lengths were then attached to the base with clear fishing line.

Small stems of feverfew, pepper berries, yarrow, lamb's ear, chive blossoms, oregano, and fraser fir were then arranged and hot-glued into the artemisia.

By botanical definition, herbs and spices encompass such a wide range of plants that the definition itself tends to be more confusing than helpful. Most of us, though, are familiar with the more traditional Christmas herbs and spices.

Most spices and culinary herbs are available in grocery stores, although you may find that some of these items are much less expensive in bulk at farmer's markets and ethnic shops. (Many Oriental markets, for instance, sell full bags of star anise for under a dollar.)

If you don't have access to some of the other herbs used in this chapter, such as artemisia and yarrow, visit the library to find an herbal mail order company. The prices are almost always reasonable and their beauty may well encourage you to plan your own herb garden this spring.

A large paper bow was first wired to the top of a grape vine base, and the bow's two streamers were woven through the grape vine down each side. Small pine cones, bay leaves, cinnamon sticks, star anise, cedar sprigs, sumac, boxwood, dried roses, caspia, and pomander balls were then arranged around the base and hot-glued in place.

Foam bases covered with crushed cinnamon are just one of the many innovative types of bases being marketed by wreath manufacturers. The cinnamon fragrance in this base is very strong when first purchased, and can be rejuvenated with a few drops of cinnamon oil as time passes and the scent fades.

For the wreath shown here, the top arrangement was created by attaching a large cotton bow with floral wire and then picking in stems of silk pine. Next, several cinnamon sticks were hot-glued around the pine, and stems of dried pepper grass, German statice, and annual statice were hot-glued around the arrangement to fill out the design.

The bottom arrangement was created with similar materials, except a pine cone and a spray of berries serve as the focal point, instead of another bow.

Christmas soaps are a fun project to make with older children during the holidays and can be fragranced with your favorite herbs and spices.

The soaps shown here were made by melting down scrap pieces of commercially-made soap and adding violet petals and a few drops of bayberry oil to the mixture before pouring it into candy molds. After the soaps have hardened, they can be decorated with herb stems, flower petals, or small hemlock cones.

Scented bath splashes are a luxurious way to lightly perfume your skin during or after your bath. When placed in decorative glass bottles, they can be displayed in a sunny window or given as gifts.

To make a bath splash, fill a one-quart jar loosely with your choice of herb stems or flower petals. Rosemary, bee balm, chamomile, roses, and violets all make nice Christmas bath splashes.

Add enough boiling water to fill the jar and allow to cool. Strain the liquid into a measuring cup and pour into your chosen bottle. For each cup of liquid, add 1⅛ teaspoons of grain alcohol. (Although whiskey and other strong alcohols work, they also dominate the gentle fragrance of flowers and herbs, so use an unscented alcohol such as vodka.)

Repeat the above process until you have enough liquid to fill the bottle. Add an herb sprig or a few flower petals if desired and a drop or two of food coloring if you'd like a darker liquid.

Note: For a more astringent bath splash, use more alcohol; for a moisturizing bath splash, add a few drops of lanolin.

Top

Spicy pomander balls decorated with ribbons and dried flowers add beauty and fragrance to Christmas trees, gift packages, and almost anywhere around the home.

Below

Five cinnamon sticks were arranged in a bundle, hot-glued together, and then decorated with dried herbs and evergreens.

Opposite page

Miniature wreath bases, baskets, and tree ornaments were decorated with an assortment of dried herbs attached with hot glue. See page 111 for more detailed directions for making the basket arrangement.

Pomander Recipe

½ cup ground cinnamon
3 tbs. ground allspice
3 tbs. ground cloves
2 tbs. ground nutmeg
2 tbs. orrisroot powder
1 cup applesauce

Combine the first five ingredients and blend well. Stir in applesauce; mix well. Roll the dough into 12 balls about the size of a walnut. If you plan to use the balls as tree ornaments, make a horizontal hole in the pomander with a crochet hook and thread with ribbon. Place the balls on a metal tray and let dry for seven to ten days, rotating occasionally.

When completely dry, decorate the balls with pieces of lace, ribbon, wire coils, and dried flowers using a glue gun. The pomanders will remain fragrant for years if stored in a covered box wrapped in tissue paper.

Although pomander balls are usually appreciated for their spicy fragrance, they can also be displayed in a special container and admired for their beauty.

Here, an antique basket was filled with fragrant evergreens and then topped with pomander balls for a beautiful table arrangement.

The pomanders were made by poking small holes in oranges with a fork and then filling them with whole cloves (available in the spice section of your grocery store) until the entire orange was covered. Apples and other citrus fruits also make wonderful pomanders.

Once the pomander is covered with cloves, it can be displayed as is, decorated with ribbons, or rolled in a mixture of powdered spices for extra fragrance. The spices usually include cinnamon, nutmeg, allspice, and cloves. Powdered orrisroot can be added if desired to help preserve the fragrance.

*T*he top two packages were decorated with evergreens, cinnamon sticks, and bay leaves. The items were hot-glued separately underneath the bows.

The bottom two packages were decorated by creating small arrangements of cones, cinnamon sticks, star anise, and pepper berries, and then securing them in place with hot glue.

This herb and spice topiary emits an enticing fragrance in a small hallway or corner.

The fragrance comes from dried tansy, star anise, cinnamon sticks, and bay leaves. Small pieces of curled grape vine, wheat stalks, dried straw-flowers, celosia, yarrow, love-in-a-mist, pepper berries, and dock were also used to add color and texture.

*The following holiday recipes
create wonderful aromas in the kitchen
without requiring a lot of time or attention.*

"Apples & Spice Compote"

*This compote smells wonderful as it's being prepared
and can be served over spice cake, vanilla ice cream,
or baked apples.*

*In medium saucepan saute 2 cups of chopped apples in
3 tablespoons of melted butter. To this mixture, gently
add ½ cup of raisins, 1 cup of apple juice, and
½ tablespoon each of cinnamon, nutmeg, and allspice
powders. Allow to simmer on low heat until the desired
consistency is reached, stirring occasionally.*

*If you'd like to keep the mixture simmering for an
extended period of time, add additional apple juice
and spices as needed.*

"Revitalizing Lemon Simmer"

*Add the following ingredients to two cups of boiling
water: sassafras, lemon thyme, lemon-scented geranium
leaves, lemon grass, lemon balm, and lemon verbena.*

*If you're not an herb gardener, these ingredients can
be located through a mail order herb supplier.*

"Mountain Herb Simmer"

*Combine small stems of cedar with lemon balm, sage,
star anise, tansy, mint leaves, cardamon, annua, and
bay leaves with two cups of boiling water.*

*Again, mail order herb suppliers are a good source
and the fragrance is well worth the effort.*

"Spicy Mulled Cider"

*Combine all ingredients except apple cider and bring
to a boil. Remove from heat, add cider, and stir well.*

*Ingredients: 1 cup water, 1 cup sugar, 1 cup dark
raisins, 5 cinnamon sticks (approximately 3 inches long),
10 whole cloves, 10 allspice berries, 1 tablespoon grated
lemon peel, 1 tablespoon grated orange peel, 1 thinly-
sliced lemon peel, 3 quarts of apple cider.*

*The cider can be served warm or refrigerated and re-
heated later.*

Opposite page

*H*olly berries, star anise, fresh boxwood, fresh cedar, bay leaves, and mosses were creatively arranged and hot-glued to a small vine base. A festive raffia bow was added last.

To store the wreath from year to year, place it in a box slightly larger than the wreath and gently cover it on all sides with tissue paper. Continue packing paper around the wreath until you do not hear any movement when you shake the box.

*I*f you've never made a wreath before and find yourself feeling a bit intimidated by the process, consider trying the method used by the designer of the wreath shown here. The designer simply gathers her materials together on a table top, experiments with their placement, and then hot-glues them to the base.

In the wreath below, the herbs and spices included bay leaves and cloves. Pine cones, dried rosebuds, and fresh cedar were used as accents.

Common & Latin Names

A

Allspice .... *Pimenta dioica*
Annual statice .... *Limonium sinuatum*
Apples .... *Malus*
Arborvitae .... *Thuja*
Artemisia .... *Artemisia*

B

Baby's breath .... *Gypsophilia elegans*
Bayberry .... *Myrica pensylvanica*
Bay .... *Laurus nobilis*
Boxwood .... *Buxus*

C

Canella berries .... *Canellaceae*
Carnations .... *Dianthus Carophyllus*
Caspia .... *Limonium caspia*
Cedar .... *Cedrus*
Celosia .... *Celosia cristata*
Chamomile .... *Chamaemelum nobile*
Chives .... *Allium Schoenoprasum*
Cinnamon .... *Cinnamomum myrianthum*
Cloves .... *Syzygium aromaticum*
Cockscomb .... *Celosia cristata*
Cornflowers .... *Centaurea Cyanus*

D

Daisies ...... *Chrysanthemum frutescens*
Delphinium .... *Delphinium*
Dianthus .... *Dianthus*
Dock .... *Rumex*
Dusty miller .... *Artemisia Stellerana*

E

Eucalyptus .... *Eucalyptus*

F

Feverfew ... *Chrysanthemum Parthenium*
Fir .... *Abies*
Fraser fir .... *Abies Fraseri*

G

German myrtle .... *Myrtus communis*
German statice .... *Limonium tatarica*
Globe amaranth ..... *Gomphrena globosa*
Gypsophilia .... *Gypsophila elegans*

H

Heather .... *Calluna*
Hemlock .... *Conium maculatum*
Holly .... *Ilex*
Hydrangea .... *Hydrangea*

J

Juniper .... *Juniperus*

L

Lamb's ear .... *Stachys byzantina*
Larkspur .... *Consolida*
Lavender .... *Lavandula*
Lemon verbena .... *Aloysia triphylla*
Love-in-a-mist .... *Nigella damascena*

Additional projects on following pages.

M

Magnolia .... *Magnolia*
Mexican sage.......... *Salvia leucantha*

N

Nutmeg............. *Myristica fragrans*

O

Oregano .... *Origanum pulchellum*
Orris ..... *Iris Xgermanica var. florentina*

P

Pearly everlasting .... *Anaphalis*
Pepper grass .... *Lepidium*
Peppermint .... *Mentha Xpiperita*
Princess pine .... *Crassula pseudolycopodloides*
Pussy willows.............. *Salix caprea*

R

Red peppers .... *Capsicum annuum*
Redwood .... *Aldenanthera pavonina*
Roses.......................... *Rosa*

S

Silver king artemisia .... *Artemisia ludoviciana*
Spruce .... *Picea*
Star anise .... *Foeniculum vulgare*
Strawflowers... *Helichrysum bracteatum*
Statice..................... *Limonium*

Sugar bush............. *Acer barbatum*
Sumac...................... *Rhus*
Sweet Annie .... *Artemisia annua*
Sweet woodruff .... *Galium odoratum*

T

Tansy .... *Tanacetum*

W

Wheat .... *Triticum Strobus*
White pine .... *Pinus*
Wormwood .... *Artemisia*

Y

Yarrow .... *Achillea*

Z

Zinnias .... *Zinnia*

Bibliography

Coffin, Tristram P.
> *The Book of Christmas Folklore.* New York City, New York: The Seabury Press, 1973.

Coon, Nelson.
> *Gardening For Fragrance Indoors And Out.* New York City, New York: Hearthside Press, Inc., 1967.

Mautor, Claudette and Rob Pulleyn.
> *Everlasting Floral Gifts.* New York City, New York: Sterling Publishing Co., 1990.

For years families have enjoyed sharing holiday evenings with creative activities such as garland-making.

This garland was made by threading sliced apples, bay leaves, cranberries, hot red peppers (dried), and drilled nutmegs onto a length of red ribbon. Each end of the garland was finished with a double-knotted loop to allow for easy hanging.

Right

Miniature Christmas trees made from cone-shaped pieces of foam (see page 20 for general directions) were simple to design and make.

The cone was first covered with sheet moss (attached with hot glue), and a row of artemisia was then spiraled down the tree, with fragrant and decorative dried materials hot-glued onto the artemisia.

The materials included cinnamon sticks, pepper berries, whole nutmegs, celosia, feverfew, oregano, tansy, chive blossoms, yarrow, lamb's ear, bay leaves, sage, and globe amaranth.

The herbal basket was made by cutting a piece of foam to fit the inside of the basket. Dried sweet Annie, artemisia, chive blossoms, feverfew, and pepper berries were then arranged and inserted into the foam by their stems.

Index